INSIDE MEN'S COLLEGE BASKETBALL™

BASKETBALL IN THE PAC-10 CONFERENCE

rosen central

JEREMY HARROW

New York

To my uncle Neil

Published in 2008 by The Rosen Publishing Group, Inc.
29 East 21st Street, New York, NY 10010

Library of Congress Cataloging-in-Publication Data

Harrow, Jeremy.
Inside men's college basketball : basketball in the Pac-10 Conference / Jeremy
Harrow. — 1st ed.
        p. cm. — (Inside men's college basketball)
Includes bibliographical references and index.
ISBN-13: 978-1-4042-1385-2 (library binding)
1. Pacific-10 Conference. 2. Basketball—West (U.S.) 3. College sports—West (U.S.)
I. Title.
GV885.415.P33H37 2008
796.323'630979—dc22

                                                                2007032647

Manufactured in the United States of America

On the cover: *(Top)* From left to right, California Golden Bears Leon Powe, Ayinde Ubaka, Richard Midgley, DeVon Hardin, and Theo Robertson stand on the court during the final moments of a semifinal win at the 2006 Pacific Life Pac-10 Men's Basketball Tournament. *(Bottom)* During a 2004 game, Josh Shipp of the UCLA Bruins (12) looks to pass around the block of Stanford Cardinal Nick Robinson (21).

CONTENTS

INTRODUCTION

College basketball has a spring fever all its own. It's called March Madness, and there's a good reason for the name. Fans, young and old, go crazy over the annual tournament that decides the national championship. There are few events in the sports world that can match the sheer excitement of watching sixty-five teams being whittled down to one. What is it about college basketball that inspires such interest? James Naismith hardly could have predicted that the game he created in 1891, as an indoor exercise for the harsh winter months, would evolve into such a phenomenon.

Naismith worked at a YMCA (Young Men's Christian Association) training school in Springfield, Massachusetts. He was developing a game suited for a gymnasium and wanted it to promote good health and teamwork. The predominant sports of the late

University of California, Los Angeles (UCLA) fans cheer during the 2006 NCAA national championship game. Some of the fans are members of the official UCLA student fan group called "the Den."

nineteenth century, such as football, baseball, and boxing, were known for their roughness. Naismith ensured that his game would keep its players apart by eliminating any bodily contact. He didn't want the ball slammed into action either. Passing would be the only acceptable form of movement. In fact, "basket ball," as it was originally spelled, was not designed to be a public spectacle. It never occurred to the game's creator that anyone would want to observe the match.

Naismith's game quickly became a hit with his students. Basketball became hugely popular, although Naismith hadn't intended to start a new craze. Many of his early students brought the game to schools all over the country. Within a few years of the sport's existence, colleges started organizing their own basketball teams. The first intercollegiate men's competition is often credited to Hamline

In Springfield, Massachusetts, Dr. James Naismith *(center row, far right)* poses with the first basketball team in history, in 1891.

College and the Minnesota State School of Agriculture. The schools played each other on February 9, 1895. Hamline's team was coached by one of Naismith's original players, Ray Kaighn.

It also didn't take long for the basketball revolution to reach the West Coast. In fact, in late 1892, a man named Walter E. Magee introduced the game to the University of California. It was actually more popular with women at first, but men soon realized the sport's potential.

The first formal association of college basketball teams took root in the Northeast among elite schools like Columbia, Cornell, Harvard, Princeton, and Yale. Now, they're known as the Ivy League, but in 1901, they called themselves the Eastern Intercollegiate Basketball League. There were no conferences yet, so they played for their own championship.

The West Coast may be more famous for its beaches and surfing, but over the years, it has made a big name for itself in men's college basketball. The Pacific Athletic Conference (Pac-10) has won seventeen national basketball championships, more than any other conference. When March Madness rolls around each year, you can always expect a team from the Pac-10 to have a serious shot at making the Final Four.

1 CHAPTER
Getting to Know the Pac-10 Conference

The Pac-10 is a Division I conference in the National Collegiate Athletic Association (NCAA). Ten western U.S. universities currently make up the conference: University of Arizona; Arizona State University; University of California, Berkeley; University of California, Los Angeles (UCLA); University of Oregon; Oregon State University; Stanford University; University of Southern California (USC); University of Washington; and Washington State University.

The majority of these schools have been playing in the same conference for more than ninety years. Their earliest association began on December 15, 1915, as the Pacific Coast Conference (PCC). The original charter members were Washington, Oregon, Oregon State, and University of California, Berkeley. By 1928, the conference had grown to ten members. Unfortunately, however, the PCC collapsed in 1959 after several football-related scandals ruined its reputation. A new conference called the Athletic Association of

Bill Walton's superior height guarantees a rebound for UCLA in a 1974 game against conference rival, USC (University of Southern California).

Western Universities took its place and eventually featured eight PCC schools. They became the Pacific Athletic Conference in 1968 and were known as the Pac-8. When Arizona and Arizona State officially joined the conference a decade later, it became the Pac-10.

Pac-10 on the Rise

The Pac-10 is a conference full of talent and winners. From 1997 to 2007, it had at least one team ranked in the nation's top 10. In 2004, Stanford ended the regular season as the number-one team in the country. The 2006–2007 season was a successful one for the Pac-10, with four nationally ranked teams (UCLA, Oregon, USC, and Washington State) in the top 25. These schools, plus Arizona and Stanford, represented the Pac-10 at the 2007 NCAA basketball tournament. It was the thirteenth time in fourteen years that the conference had at least four teams in the tournament. (Six teams was a Pac-10 record, a feat also accomplished in 2002.) Only Oregon, the Pac-10 tournament champion, received an automatic bid to the NCAA tournament. The other five teams were chosen based on their season's winning records.

UCLA

UCLA's most impressive statistic may be its sheer number of first-round NBA (National Basketball Association) draft picks. In 2007, Arron Afflalo became the twenty-ninth Bruin ever to be chosen in the first round. The Bruins are arguably the greatest team in college basketball history. Since 1964, they have won eleven national titles, more than any other Division I team. They won seven of these NCAA championships

UCLA's Arron Afflalo shoots over Florida Gator Lee Humphrey during the 2006 NCAA championship game. Afflalo helped lead UCLA back to the Final Four in 2007.

in a row. It was just one of the Bruins' many record-breaking winning streaks. They also had an eighty-eight-game winning streak that stretched from 1971 to 1974. From 1962 to 1979, UCLA won seventeen out of eighteen conference championships. Thanks to legendary coach John Wooden, UCLA was the most dominating team ever to step on the court. They have remained one of the best teams in the country since the Wooden era. Although the Bruins' last championship was in 1995, coach Ben Howland guided the 2006 and 2007 teams to the Final Four.

Oregon

Oregon captured its only national championship at the very first NCAA tournament, in 1939. In their history, the Ducks have won only four conference championships. However, Oregon fans felt the excitement again when the Ducks earned the Pac-10 title in 2002 for the first time in almost sixty years. They also won the Pac-10 tournament championship in 2003 and 2007.

Head coach Ernie Kent once played on another great Oregon squad in the mid-1970s. He was part of a tough-as-nails group called the Kamikaze Kids. (They got their nickname as a result of their constant hustle and by using their bodies like guided missiles.) Since taking over in 1997, Kent has reformed Oregon. The Ducks made it to the Elite Eight of the NCAA tournament in 2002 and 2007. Kent recruited future NBA players Aaron Brooks, Fred Jones, Luke Jackson, and Luke Ridnour.

Washington State

Washington State's only national championship was in 1917, before a postseason tournament existed. They were the first school from the Pac-10 ever to win a basketball championship. The Cougars also played in the 1941 championship game against Wisconsin. The only two years that Washington State finished first in the conference were 1917 and 1941. However, in 2007, the Cougars finished in second place behind UCLA, with a 26–8 overall record. The team made it to the second round of the 2007 NCAA tournament. This was a miraculous turnaround for a team that had finished last the previous season. The man who took Washington State from nowhere to a place among the Pac-10's best was a rookie coach named

Washington State coach Tony Bennett confers with one of his players, Mac Hopson, during the 2007 Pac-10 tournament. Bennett took over the Cougars' coaching job from his father, Dick Bennett, who retired in 2006.

Tony Bennett. For his achievement, Bennett received the National Coach of the Year award.

USC

USC has won seven conference championships over the years, earning its last title in 1985. The Trojans also made Final Four appearances in 1940 and 1954. USC has finished ten seasons as a top-ranked team in the country. As with most teams in the Pac-10, the Trojans have often

CURRENT PAC-10 TEAMS AND THEIR ACCOMPLISHMENTS

SCHOOL	TEAM NAME	YEAR JOINED PAC-10	ALL-TIME REGULAR SEASON CONFERENCE CHAMPIONSHIPS	PAC-10 TOURNAMENT TITLES	NCAA TOURNAMENT APPEARANCES
University of Arizona	Wildcats	1978	11	4	26
Arizona State University	Sun Devils	1978	0	0	12
University of California, Berkeley	Golden Bears	1959	14	0	14
University of California, Los Angeles (UCLA)	Bruins	1959	29	2	41
University of Oregon	Ducks	1964	4	2	9
Oregon State University	Beavers	1964	12	0	16
University of Southern California (USC)	Trojans	1959	7	0	13
Stanford University	Cardinal	1959	11	1	14
University of Washington	Huskies	1959	10	1	13
Washington State University	Cougars	1962	2	0	5

played in the shadow of their state rival, UCLA. This was especially true in the early 1970s, when UCLA was winning one NCAA crown after another. USC ranked in the top twenty in 1970, 1971, 1974, and 1975. In 1971, the Trojans were 24–2 and the number-five team in the country. USC brought its success into the new millennium when it was once again among Division I's top teams in 2002 and 2007. Since 2000, Trojan players Nick Young, Gabe Pruitt, Sam Clancy, Brian Scalabrine, and Jeff Trepagnier have all been drafted into the NBA.

Arizona

Arizona is becoming every bit as great as rival UCLA. The Wildcats joined the conference in 1978 but already have eleven Pac-10

NCAA TOURNAMENT WINS/LOSSES (winning percentage)	NCAA FINAL FOUR APPEARANCES	NCAA CHAMPIONSHIPS	PAC-10 CONFERENCE PLAYERS OF THE YEAR	FIRST-ROUND NBA DRAFT PICKS
41–25 (.621)	4	1	6	13
12–13 (.480)	0	0	2	7
18–14 (.563)	3	1	4	8
94–34 (.734)	17	11	6	29
12–8 (.600)	1	1	3	11
12–19 (.387)	2	0	5	12
11–15 (.423)	2	0	3	7
19–14 (.576)	2	1	1	9
14–14 (.500)	1	0	2	7
4–5 (.444)	1	0	1	1

championships. Arizona is also a four-time Pac-10 tournament champion. Since Lute Olson took over as head coach in 1983, Arizona has played in twenty-four consecutive NCAA tournaments. It won its only national championship in 1997 after defeating three number-one seeds. It also made it to the Final Four in 1988, 1994, and 2001. Arizona is almost always one of the top teams in college basketball. As of 2007, Arizona had won twenty or more games for twenty consecutive years. The Wildcats also won thirty or more games in 1988, 1998, and 2005. What really sets the Wildcats apart from other Pac-10 teams is the number of Arizona players who went on to become NBA stars. Former Wildcats include Steve Kerr, Sean Elliot, Mike Bibby, Damon Stoudamire, Gilbert Arenas, Luke Walton, Jason Terry, and Richard Jefferson.

Great Coaches of the Pac-10

The Pac-10 has almost as many coaches in the Basketball Hall of Fame as it has players. Two of the biggest names ever to coach college basketball are Pac-10 legends John Wooden and Lute Olson. There are eight active and former Pac-10 coaches with 500 or more Division I wins. These coaches know how to get the best out of their teams, and their jobs are never done. There are always practice drills to run, game films to watch, new plays to think about, and fresh talent to recruit.

John Wooden

UCLA coach John Wooden understood great players because he used to be one. In 1932, Wooden was a guard for national champion Purdue. He went on to coach the UCLA Bruins from 1948 to 1975. His 885 career wins over forty seasons as a coach are still among

John Wooden rallies his troops during a break in the semifinals of the 1970 NCAA tournament. Wooden retired from coaching in 1975 but continued to inspire others as an author and motivational speaker.

the highest in basketball history. Wooden collected 620 of those wins at UCLA, a conference record. What's even more amazing is that he lost only 147 games at UCLA! The Bruins' eighty-eight-game winning streak from 1971 to 1974 is the best of all time. Wooden's winning percentage (.804) ranks third on the all-time Division I coaches list. Furthermore, his ten NCAA championships is a record that no one else has come close to matching. The fact that Wooden won seven of them in row has made him a living legend. UCLA also won thirty-eight straight NCAA tournament games, completely dominating the sport.

Wooden's teams owned the Pac-10. They took home sixteen conference trophies during his twenty-seven years at the school. During the late 1960s and early 1970s, the team had a little help from two very big people. Kareem Abdul-Jabbar (then known as Lew Alcindor), at 7 feet, 2 inches (2.19 meters), and Bill Walton, standing 7 feet (2.13 m) tall, towered over their opponents as UCLA centers. Wooden designed his offense to get the ball in their hands at the right moments. He also used these two future NBA Hall of Famers to open up scoring opportunities for their teammates. John Wooden has the special distinction of being the first person ever inducted into the Naismith Basketball Hall of Fame as both a player and a coach.

Ralph Miller

Ralph Miller, who coached Oregon State from 1971 to 1989, reminded the world that there were other teams in the Pac-10 besides UCLA. Using Miller's "pressure defense" system to wear down opponents, the Beavers took over the conference with a 49–5 record against Pac-10 rivals. They won four Pac-10 championships, winning three straight from 1980 to 1982. The Beavers got their first ever number-one ranking in 1981 and didn't finish a season ranked lower than number five during the three-year period. The 1981 team got everyone's attention by winning twenty-six consecutive games. The Beavers capped off their remarkable three-year run with a 77–11 overall record. Miller won back-to-back National Coach of the Year awards in 1981 and 1982. He was inducted into the Naismith Hall of Fame in 1988 and retired from college basketball with 674 wins.

Lute Olson crouches next to his bench of Arizona players during a 2003 NCAA tournament game against Kansas. When he was in college, Olson played basketball at Augsburg College in Minnesota.

Lute Olson

Lute Olson, who has been coaching Arizona basketball since 1983, walks in John Wooden's footsteps as a man who knows how to win. As of 2007, the Wildcats' leader was in second place among active coaches for Division I victories, with 780. A coach who wins that many games also wins a lot of awards. Olson is a two-time National Coach of the Year and a seven-time Pac-10 Coach of the Year. His accomplishments at Arizona speak for themselves: eleven Pac-10 championships and one national championship (1997). The secret to Olson's success is his ability to recruit the finest high school players. He has a sharp eye for great point guards. NBA stars Mike Bibby, Jason Terry, Damon Stoudamire, and Gilbert Arenas all excelled at running the court for Arizona. The NBA draft has been very good to Olson's players. More than thirty of his former Wildcats have been drafted into the pros. Lute Olson was inducted into the Naismith Basketball Hall of Fame in 2002.

Mike Montgomery

A John R. Wooden Lifetime Achievement Award is a huge honor. Mike Montgomery, who coached at Stanford from 1986 to 2004, was presented with the prestigious award in 2004. He is simply the greatest basketball coach in Stanford history. Montgomery's career record at the school (393–167) is unmatched by his predecessors. In his eighteen years with the Cardinal (the team is named after one of the school's colors, a shade of red), he had only one losing season. Under Montgomery, Stanford joined UCLA and Arizona as the premier teams of the Pac-10. The Cardinal was among the nation's top-ranked teams from 1997 to 2004. Stanford won the 1991 National Invitation Tournament (NIT) after not seeing the postseason in decades. Montgomery brought four Pac-10 championships (1999, 2000, 2001, 2004) to a school that was used to being at the bottom. The only thing Montgomery didn't win at Stanford was an NCAA title, although his team took twelve trips to the NCAA tournament. They got as far as the Final Four in 1998. Montgomery's last season, 2004–2005, turned out to be his finest one ever. Stanford went 30–2 and finished the regular season as the number-one-ranked

Mike Montgomery outlines a strategy for his Stanford players during a time-out in a 2003 game. Montgomery resigned from Stanford after the 2004 season to coach the NBA's Golden State Warriors.

team in the country. Montgomery then left Stanford to coach the San Francisco Warriors in the NBA.

Ben Braun

In 1996, Ben Braun came to rescue a California basketball team that was stuck in controversy. The previous coach, Todd Bozeman, was banned from the NCAA for recruiting violations. Braun helped California bounce back with a sensational year (23–9) in 1997. The Golden Bears finished second in the Pac-10 and made it to the Sweet Sixteen in the NCAA tournament. As a result, Braun won Pac-10

California coach Ben Braun talks with Amit Tamir during a 2003 NCAA tournament game. Braun coached Eastern Michigan before coming to the Golden Bears.

Coach of the Year honors, becoming the first California coach to do so.

Ever since, Braun has steadily built the Golden Bears into an impressive program. California has seen more winning seasons than losing ones since he took over. In fact, in Braun's first ten years, California had six seasons of twenty wins or more. They also made five appearances in the NCAA tournament. In 1999, California also surprised their fans with an NIT championship. It was the team's first postseason title in forty years. The Golden Bears have yet to reach the levels of UCLA or Arizona, but they are well on their way. With a 202–138 record under Braun, California likely will be a threat for years to come.

3 CHAPTER

Great Players of the Pac-10

Every decade, the Pac-10 has produced a new generation of future NBA All-Stars. In 2007, the NBA selected six Pac-10 players among the first thirty-three picks of the draft. Many careers are started in the Pac-10 because of the high level of competition. Pac-10 players always attract interest because of their court smarts. They know exactly how to pass, shoot, steal, and rebound the ball to shut down their rivals.

Lew Alcindor

Lew Alcindor—as he was known before changing his name to Kareem Abdul-Jabbar—was every college coach's dream. The 7 foot, 2 inch (2.19 m) center could shoot, rebound, and block the ball over everyone else's heads. He was also extremely fast. It was nearly impossible to stop him. Alcindor came to UCLA in 1965 and helped

UCLA legend Lew Alcindor (#33) shoots a basket during a 1967 Final Four game against Houston. Alcindor became famous for his "Skyhook" shot, which he could shoot from either side.

build the greatest dynasty in college basketball history. UCLA went 88–2 during his three years on the team. The Bruins won three straight NCAA championships with their unstoppable center. Alcindor won the Most Outstanding Player award for all three NCAA tournaments. (He is the only player ever to win it three times!) He completed his UCLA career with 2,325 points and 1,367 rebounds. The Milwaukee Bucks selected Alcindor with the first pick of the 1969 NBA draft. Alcindor changed his name to Kareem Abdul-Jabbar after converting to Islam. Abdul-Jabbar retired in 1989 as the all-time leading scorer in the NBA with 38,387 points. He was inducted into the Naismith Basketball Hall of Fame in 1995.

Bill Walton

When Lew Alcindor left UCLA, John Wooden didn't have to wait long to find a replacement for the Bruins' big man. Bill Walton arrived in 1970 with two California state championships on his high school resume. The talented 7-footer (2.13 m) could shoot, pass, block, rebound, and intimidate the other teams. Despite numerous injuries, he threw his body around, making him tough against opponents. Walton helped continue UCLA's

Bill Walton shoots during the 1973 NCAA championship game. His 44 points against Memphis State were a championship-game record.

epic winning streak with three more NCAA Championships (1972–1974). He scored 44 points in a near-perfect shooting performance during the 1973 title game against Memphis State. In his three years as a Bruin, Walton averaged 20.3 points and 15.7 rebounds per game. He won every award possible all three years: All-Pac-8, All-American, Pac-8 Player of the Year, and NCAA Player of the Year. The Portland Trailblazers chose him as the number-one pick in the 1974 NBA draft. Walton was inducted into the Naismith Basketball Hall of Fame in 1993.

Superfast Gary Payton goes for a layup during his days as an All-Star guard for Oregon State. Payton went on to play for the NBA's Seattle Supersonics.

Gary Payton

Gary Payton's determination on the court led him to an all-American career at Oregon State. Payton played for the Beavers from 1987 to 1990, under Hall of Fame coach Ralph Miller. Payton was Miller's greatest player and started every game for four years. He was a double threat because he was dangerous on both sides of the court. As a defender, Payton was relentless on man-to-man coverage and a master at stealing the ball. He holds the school record with 321 steals. When he got the ball, Payton immediately doubled his team's chances of scoring a basket. He is Oregon State's all-time leader in scoring (2,172 points) and assists (938). The 6-foot, 4-inch (1.95 m) point guard averaged 25.7 points, 8.1 assists, 4.7 rebounds, and 3.4 steals per game. Payton's high-flying numbers in 1990 helped make Oregon State a Pac-10 champion for the first time in six years. He was the Pac-10 Player of the Year and the second pick in the first round of the 1990 NBA draft.

Jason Kidd

Every basketball fan knows Jason Kidd as the All-Star point guard for the New Jersey Nets. Kidd, however, was once an all-American point guard for the California Golden Bears. He played two outstanding seasons at California before jumping to the pros. He made the All-Pac-10 team as a freshman, in 1993, when he averaged 13 points, 7.7 assists, and 3.8 steals per game. His 110 steals that year set a single-season Pac-10 record. California made two consecutive NCAA tournament appearances with Kidd. In

California's Jason Kidd demonstrates his skill as one of the greatest passers to ever play in the Pac-10. Kidd was the second overall pick in the 1994 NBA draft.

1993, he made national headlines when California upset heavily favored Duke in the second round of the tournament. California went 22–8 in 1994, and Kidd was the top passer in the NCAA with 9.1 assists per game. He became the first sophomore ever to be voted Pac-10 Player of the Year. Although he stayed only two years, Kidd's impact on Golden Bears basketball will never be forgotten. He holds school records for career steals (204) and assists in a season (272).

Mike Bibby

Mike Bibby, who played for Arizona from 1996 to 1998, was destined for greatness as a point guard. His father, Henry Bibby, was the starting point guard for three UCLA championship teams (1970–1972). He inherited his father's talent and put it to good use. As a freshman, Bibby averaged 13.5 points and 5.2 assists per game. He also became a hero for the Wildcats in the postseason. His 19 points, 9 rebounds, and 4 assists in a thrilling title-game victory over Kentucky helped the Wildcats win the 1997 NCAA championship. As a result, Bibby was the 1997 Pac-10 Freshman of the Year. In 1998, he averaged 17.2 points, 5.7 assists, and 2.4 steals per game. He helped lead Arizona to a 30–5 record and a Pac-10 championship. He was named the Pac-10 Player of the Year after the Wildcats lost in the NCAA quarterfinals. Bibby decided to go pro after his sophomore year, and the Vancouver Grizzlies selected him with the second pick of the draft.

Pac-10 Award Winners

The following Pac-10 athletes have won some of the most prestigious national awards that are given away each year.

Naismith Men's College Player of the Year Award (awarded since 1969)
Lew Alcindor, UCLA, 1969
Bill Walton, UCLA, 1972, 1973, 1974
Marques Johnson, UCLA, 1977

Oscar Robertson Trophy (College Player of Year Award since 1959)
Walt Hazzard, UCLA, 1964
Lew Alcindor, UCLA, 1967, 1968
Sidney Wicks, UCLA, 1971
Bill Walton, UCLA, 1972, 1973, 1974
Marques Johnson, UCLA, 1977

Ed O'Bannon, UCLA, 1995

Adolph Rupp Trophy (College Player of Year award since 1972)
Bill Walton, UCLA, 1972, 1973, 1974
Marques Johnson, UCLA 1977
Sean Elliott, Arizona, 1989

John R. Wooden Player of the Year (awarded since 1976)
Marques Johnson, UCLA, 1977
Sean Elliott, Arizona, 1989
Ed O'Bannon, UCLA, 1995

4 CHAPTER

Games of the Pac-10

College basketball is all about the games, and there are a lot of them. Including regular and postseason, most Division I teams will play around thirty games. A long season allows a team to experiment with different lineups and strategies. It gives each player time to develop on the court. It also means that a losing streak does not necessarily ruin a team's chances for the postseason. There's enough time to make mistakes and learn from them. On the other hand, a team can lose its momentum halfway through the season and never get it back. This is why the preseason favorites are not always the same teams that make headlines during March Madness.

Regular Season

Every game in the regular season is a stepping stone to the postseason. Each team wants a bid to the NCAA tournament. At the end

Oregon defeated California, 83–61, on its way to winning the 2007 Pac-10 tournament. Above, Golden Bears' Alex Pribble (31) shoots between two Oregon "Ducks."

of the regular season, the NCAA evaluates the schools' results. Besides getting a bid, teams also want to get as high a seed as possible. The highest seeds will play the weakest opponents (lowest seeds) in the first round of the tournament. Being highly seeded is a sign of respect and recognition of a team's elite status. It can also translate into more exposure in the press. This can help a school to not only recruit the best high school talent, but also to increase the number of admissions applications from across the country.

The regular season generally starts in November and finishes around the end of February. In addition to playing against all the other teams in its conference, a school will also play a select number of non-conference opponents. These other games are very important. They give the team a chance to measure itself against squads from other parts of the country. A school that finishes in fourth or fifth place in a tough conference will get special consideration if it played well against non-conference teams with better records.

Postseason Tournaments

When the regular season ends, the postseason takes over. The teams in the Pac-10 first fight it out in the Pacific Life Pac-10 Tournament. This tournament is relatively new. It began in 1987 but was discontinued in 1990, when the Pac-10 decided that it wasn't getting enough attention from the fans or the media. The conference eventually reinstated the tournament in 2002. The winner of the Pac-10 tournament automatically advances to the NCAA tournament. Other conference teams that excelled during the regular season and in the Pac-10 tournament are also invited to play. In the NCAA tournament, sixty-five teams battle it out for the national championship. (The NCAA tournament began in 1939, with eight teams. It has since expanded to sixty-five.) The two lowest-ranked teams compete a week before the conference to see who will go on to the first elimination round. After two rounds of the tournament, sixteen teams remain, or the Sweet Sixteen. The next round becomes the Elite Eight, and then it's down to the Final Four. The winners of the Final Four advance to the championship game.

Home Games

Home games are exciting opportunities to express school spirit. Painted faces, cheerleaders, pep bands, and mischievous mascots are all part of the fun. These games are also important for the players, who need their fans' support. They need to hear the thunderous applause every time they sink a basket. It helps them build confidence, and that translates into a better performance. In addition, the fans' noise can make it a lot harder for the opposition to make

Hometown fans offer enthusiastic support to their team—and try to distract visiting players. Above, Oregon's rowdy "Pit Crew" uses a cutout of the *Star Wars* character Chewbacca to try to mock California player Ayinde Ubaka's last name.

free throws. Any distraction may work against the other team. It's called the "home-court advantage."

Pauley Pavilion

No other arena in the Pac-10 has seen more wins, championships, and future Hall of Famers than UCLA's Pauley Pavilion. The 12,819-seat facility was built in 1965, as the Bruins were beginning their golden era. They were nearly unbeatable at home for the next ten years. The Bruins were 40–0 at the arena from 1965 to 1968. USC became the first Pac-10 team ever to beat UCLA at Pauley, on March 8, 1969. It was a thrilling 46–44 upset. It would be another six years before UCLA would lose again at home. The team went on an unbelievable 98–0 run from 1970 to 1975.

By 2000, the Bruins had amassed a whopping 500 home victories. UCLA has continued its tradition of domination at Pauley over 2006 and 2007, with a 34–3 record. The famous venue has also been home to many other premier sports and entertainment events, such as the 1984 Olympics and the 1992 MTV Music Video Awards.

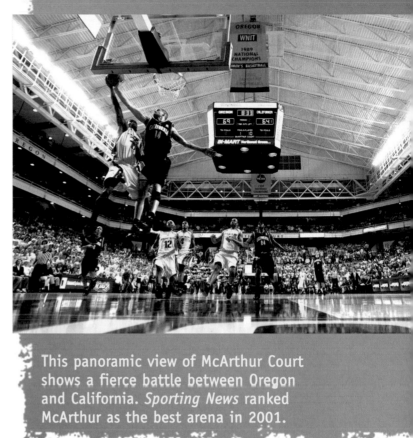

This panoramic view of McArthur Court shows a fierce battle between Oregon and California. *Sporting News* ranked McArthur as the best arena in 2001.

McArthur Court

Oregon's McArthur Court is one of the oldest, smallest, and scariest arenas in college basketball. For the visiting team, it is like playing in front of an angry mob. Friends and foes call McArthur "the Pit." The fearsome facility seats only 9,087 people, but it feels like twice that number when the fans start yelling. McArthur opened in 1926, and its design leaves little space between the fans and the players. Students generally sit courtside, but three balconies of roaring

Ducks fans also hover over the action. Winning season or not, the Ducks almost always play to a full house. There have been some great moments for Oregon's faithful. In 2001–2002, the Ducks were undefeated at Mac Court (16–0). In 1974 and 2007, the maple floor of McArthur was also the sight of two stunning upsets over then number-one-ranked UCLA.

Maples Pavilion

No other school in the Pac-10 uses its sports facility quite as effectively as Stanford. The Maples Pavilion features a court made of maple wood, which acts as both a cushion and a springboard for the players' feet. The Cardinal set a school record by winning twenty consecutive home games at Maples from 1997 to 1998. They outscored their opponents by 23.8 points per game during that streak.

As much a part of the game as the starting lineup are the Cardinal fans. Maples is even smaller than Oregon's McArthur Court, with only 7,391 seats. It's also widely believed to be the loudest arena in the conference. Cardinal fans take their role as intimidators very seriously. They will scream, shout, stand, and shake the building for the entire game. Stanford created the "Sixth Man" in 1994 to give their rabid fans a real identity. (The nickname comes from the fact that a team is allowed only five starting players on the court at a time. Therefore, the "Sixth Man" is the next best player.) The Sixth Man club is made up entirely of students who sit mid-court, wearing special T-shirts. Their job is to rattle the visiting team's nerves, and they're very good at it. Stanford also has an enthusiastic pep band. The band keeps the music going at high decibels to contribute to the raucous atmosphere.

Haas Pavilion

When the California Golden Bears' opponents enter Haas Pavilion, they better be ready to face 900 rowdy students who sit courtside. These students are known as "the Bench," and they are experts at heckling the visiting team. Although they have seats, they never actually sit in them. Everybody in the stands wears blue and gold, the school colors. The Straw Hat Band sits right under one of the baskets to

California's Straw Hat Band marches in a victory parade after the Golden Bears defeat Stanford at Haas Pavilion.

distract the opposition. The combined volume of the Bench and the band can be heard outside the arena. Haas Pavilion was built on top of the old Harmon Gym in 1999. The 11,877 seats hang over the court at high angles so there are no blind spots.

No Pac-10 team dreads the wrath of those 11,877 fans more than Stanford. The Cardinal and the Golden Bears have a long-standing rivalry that dates back to the late nineteenth century. On February 9, 2006, California ended a three-year losing streak against Stanford, winning 65–62. The Golden Bears sank six free throws in the final minute during one of the best showdowns ever in Haas Pavilion.

5 CHAPTER

Mascots and Traditions of the Pac-10

The Pac-10 mascots are easily recognizable to college basketball fans everywhere. Although the oversized figures are familiar, not everyone knows the history behind each one. There are a lot of different reasons for team nicknames. Animal nicknames are the most popular in team sports. The Pac-10 has seven teams with animal mascots. Other teams are named after a fictional character or just a simple color.

Arizona Wildcats

The real bobcats that roam through Arizona inspired the school's nickname. Arizona's first mascot, in 1915, was a wild bobcat named Rufus Arizona. The school continued using real bobcats for another fifty years before debuting their costumed mascot, Wilbur, in 1959. Wilbur's wife, Wilma, joined the Arizona family in 1986.

Arizona's most beloved tradition is its popular cheer called "Bear Down." These two words were the last words of a student athlete named John Salmon. He was fatally injured in a car accident during the 1926 season. According to the Arizona Wildcats' official Web site, Salmon's final message to his baseball teammates was, "Tell them . . . tell the team to bear down."

Arizona State Sun Devils

Arizona State's mischievous Sun Devil is the third mascot in the history of the school. Arizona State was originally

Arizona's Wilbur the Wildcat charges across the court with the school flag during a 2003 Pac-10 tournament game.

called Tempe Normal, and its name was the Owls. Tempe Normal became Arizona State Teachers College in 1925. The "Owls" then became "Bulldogs." It wasn't until 1946 that the school now known as Arizona State University adopted its current nickname. The alumni and students felt that there were already too many Bulldogs in the NCAA. They wanted a symbol that was more unique. The student body agreed upon Sun Devils. The Sun Devil mascot is called Sparky. A former Disney artist named Bert Anthony created Sparky's image.

California Golden Bears

The Golden Bears name is a combination of two powerful symbols associated with California. California is known as the Golden State because of the famous gold rush that brought people there in the mid-nineteenth century. The grizzly bear is the official state animal. In 1895, the two symbols came together at the University of California, in Berkely's mascot. A special banner was designed that year to accompany the track and field team on a national tour. The banner was illustrated with a golden grizzly bear. The school used live bears at games until 1940. A costumed bear named Oski took over the official mascot duties in 1941.

Oregon Ducks

The mascot for the Oregon Ducks is none other than Donald Duck! Oregon obtained special permission from Walt Disney in 1947 to use the famous cartoon character. The arrangement with Disney ended the practice of having live ducks at games. The idea of the mascot began with an old state nickname. Oregon was known as the Webfoot State because it rained often. The students began to call themselves "webfoots" or "webfooters." The Ducks became the official nickname in 1932 after a student vote. Another election in 1978 reaffirmed Donald as the permanent face of Oregon athletics.

Oregon State Beavers

Oregon is famous for being the Beaver State. Therefore, the beaver was the most obvious choice for Oregon State's mascot. The school's archives suggest the name first appeared between 1910 and 1916.

Previous mascots included a coyote, a bulldog, and an avid fan named John Richard Newton Bell. Oregon State used real beavers until a costumed beaver took over the role in 1952. The beaver's name has changed several times. The first one was called Beavo. Other beavers were called Billy. The students in the 1940s began calling him Benny, which has been the mascot's name ever since. Benny's image was updated in 2001 (he now looks more fierce).

Benny Beaver proudly wears his Oregon State uniform while interacting with the crowd. Oregon State students refer to Benny as the "Angry Beaver."

Stanford Cardinal

Stanford has the most unusual nickname in the Pac-10. Its teams are known as the Cardinal. Cardinal is a reference to one of its team colors, a vivid shade of red. Stanford's athletic teams were called the Indians from 1930 to 1972. When this name became offensive to its Native American students, a long debate followed regarding what should replace it. The school eventually decided to use the cardinal color to represent all of its teams. There is no official mascot for the Cardinal. The "Tree," however, a member of the Stanford Band, is a fan favorite at games.

UCLA Bruins

UCLA's earliest mascots were live bears. Costumed mascots took over—Joe and Josephine Bruin have been working the court together since 1967.

UCLA's furry mascot has always been a bear. The first athletes were called Cubs. This nickname was short-lived, however, as the student body wanted a more ferocious symbol. UCLA therefore became the Grizzlies in 1924. Unfortunately, the new name lasted only two years. The school had to give it up when it joined the Pacific Coast Conference, since the University of Montana had already claimed the name. The California Golden Bears were then also using the name "Bruins," which means "bears." The students at California agreed to offer UCLA the Bruins name. Beginning in the mid-1960s, costumed mascot Joe Bruin appeared at UCLA games. Josephine Bruin soon joined him.

USC Trojans

The Trojans have one of the most famous nicknames in NCAA history. USC's warrior mascot is a tribute to the fighting spirit of its teams. (Trojans were citizens of a mythological city called Troy, and they were enemies of the ancient Greeks. Their ten-year war with the

Tommy Trojan performs in front of USC cheerleaders during an intermission at the 2003 Pac-10 tournament championship game against Oregon.

Greeks was described in a famous poem called *The Iliad*.) The name was given to the school in 1912 by a sportswriter named Owen Bird. He described USC as Trojans because the team showed courage against bigger and better teams. USC has a special basketball mascot, called Tommy Trojan. He runs onto the court in full battle uniform waving the USC flag. Tommy is based on a bronze Trojan statue in the middle of the school's campus. The statue was built in 1930 to commemorate USC's fiftieth anniversary.

Washington Huskies

Washington's original nickname was unusual. In 1919, the students decided to call themselves the Sun Dodgers. Campus officials were not happy with the name. They wanted a symbol that reflected the rugged nature of the Northwest. The athletic department began calling themselves Vikings while a committee determined the final choices. They ultimately narrowed it down to "Malamutes" and "Huskies." The final vote favored the Huskies, an appropriate nickname for a school close to the wild frontier. Huskies are thick-furred dogs that are native to Siberia in Northern Asia. They have great stamina, and they work well in packs.

Washington State Cougars

Cougars live in the dense wilderness around the Northwest. It was a 1919 football game against California that inspired the school's nickname. Washington State defeated California so easily that a newspaper cartoonist drew them as a cougar overpowering a bear. The first mascot was a real cougar cub named Butch, who was named after a popular Washington football player, Herbert "Butch" Meeker. The governor of Washington donated the cougar cub in 1927. Future governors continued this tradition for another fifty years. The only mountain lion on campus these days, however, is a costumed mascot called Butch T. Cougar.

GLOSSARY

alumni Graduates of a particular school or college.

assist When a player passes the ball to an open teammate, who then scores a basket.

bid An invitation to compete in a postseason tournament.

bruin A bear.

campus The land and buildings of a school or college.

center The player who holds the middle position near the basket to score, rebound, and block shots. He is usually the tallest player on the team.

conference A group of schools in a close geographic area that compete against each other in different sports.

defense The act of preventing one's opponent from scoring any points.

draft The annual selection process by which NBA teams select players from colleges, high schools, or foreign countries.

dynasty When one team wins many championships over a long period of time.

elite The group or groups regarded as being the best.

Elite Eight The final eight teams in the NCAA Division I Basketball Tournament, which compete in the regional finals.

facility A building created to serve a particular function, such as hosting athletic events.

Final Four The final four teams in the NCAA Division I Basketball Tournament.

forward In basketball, there are two forward positions, the power forward and the small forward. The power forward is the bigger, stronger forward who plays close to the basket and is responsible for rebounding and inside scoring. The small forward is usually versatile enough to play near the basket or shoot from the outside.

free throw An uncontested shot worth one point. Free throws are taken from a special line fifteen feet from the basket after a foul or violation has been committed.

inducted Officially admitted into a Hall of Fame.

intimidate In basketball, to use advantages like height or weight to scare off an opponent.

malamute A sled dog of northern North America.

offense The act of scoring as many points as possible for the team.

pavilion A building open for exhibits or events.

phenomenon Someone or something that is very unusual or extraordinary.

point guard The player who brings the ball up the court with the shooting guard. The point guard does most of the ball handling while setting up the offense.

predominant Having authority or influence over others.

premier Important in size or quality.

prestigious Someone or something that is impressive or influential.

raucous Loud or rowdy.

rebound When a player gains possession of the ball after it misses the basket or bounces off the backboard.

seed A rank given to each team in the NCAA Division I Basketball Tournament based on its overall record.

shooting guard The second guard who takes the majority of the shots from the outside, especially from the three-point line.

spectacle A remarkable sight or a large public display.

Sweet Sixteen The final sixteen teams in the NCAA Division I Basketball Tournament.

undergraduate A college student who has not yet graduated from his or her school.

FOR MORE INFORMATION

Naismith International Basketball Foundation (NIBF)
120 Arrowhead Lane
North Barrington, IL 60010
(847) 277-7306
Web site: http://www.green-room-web-design.com/
  naismith%20foundation/Concept%20I/index.html
The NIBF was established in 1998 with the mission to restore, preserve, and promote the game's spirit of fun, respect, fair play, and teamwork.

Naismith Memorial Basketball Hall of Fame
1000 West Columbus Avenue
Springfield, MA 01105
(877) 4HOOPLA (446-6752) or (413) 781-6500
Web site: http://www.hoophall.com
The Naismith Memorial Basketball Hall of Fame is dedicated to promoting and preserving the history of the game of basketball.

National Collegiate Athletic Association (NCAA)
700 W. Washington Street
P.O. Box 6222
Indianapolis, IN 46206-6222
(317) 917-6222
Web site: http://www.ncaa.org
The NCAA is the governing body for every collegiate sport in the United States.

Pacific Athletic Conference (Pac-10)
1350 Treat Boulevard, Suite 500

Walnut Creek, CA 94597-8853

(925) 932-4411

Web site: http://www.pac-10.org

The Pac-10 conference, made up of ten universities, sponsors eleven men's sports and eleven women's sports.

Youth Basketball of America

10325 Orangewood Boulevard

Orlando, FL 32821

(407) 363-9262

Web site: http://www.yboa.org

Youth Basketball of America is an international governing body that promotes youth basketball worldwide.

Web Sites

Due to the changing nature of Internet links, Rosen Publishing has developed an online list of Web sites related to the subject of this book. This site is updated regularly. Please use this link to access the list:

http://www.rosenlinks.com/imcb/bptc

FOR FURTHER READING

DeCock, Luke. *Great Teams in College Basketball History* (Great Teams). Chicago, IL: Raintree, 2006.

DeVenzio, Dick. *Stuff Good Players Should Know: Intelligent Basketball from A to Z*. Austin, TX: Bridgeway Books, 2006.

Howard-Cooper, Scott. *The Bruin 100: The Greatest Games in the History of UCLA Basketball*. Lenexa, KS: Addax Publishing, 2002.

Rappoport, Ken. *Jason Kidd: Leader on the Court* (Sports Leaders). Berkeley Heights, NJ: Enslow Publishers, 2004.

Sporting News. *Sporting News Selects Legends of College Basketball*. New York, NY: McGraw-Hill, 2002.

Stewart, Mark. *The Final Four* (The Watts History of Sports). Danbury, CT: Franklin Watts, 2002.

BIBLIOGRAPHY

"Bill Walton: Biography." Retrieved June 12, 2007 (http://www.billwalton.com/bio.html).

Broido, Bing. *Spalding Book of Rules*. Indianapolis, IN: Masters Press, 1997.

Brown, Gerry, and Michael Morrison, eds. *2007 ESPN Sports Almanac*. New York, NY: ESPN Books, 2006.

CalBears.com. "Ben Braun Profile." "Traditions: Golden Bears." Retrieved June 2007 (http://calbears.cstv.com).

"The Duck." GoDucks.com. Retrieved June 15, 2007 (http://www.goducks.com/ViewArticle.dbml?DB_OEM_ID=500&ATCLID=153778).

Fournier, Peter J. *The Handbook of Mascots & Nicknames*. Lithia, FL: Raja & Associates, 2004.

GoStanford.com. "Mike Montgomery Profile." "What Is the History of Stanford's Mascot and Nickname?" Retrieved June 2007 (http://gostanford.cstv.com).

Hickok, Ralph. *The Encyclopedia of North American Sports History*. 2nd ed. New York, NY: Facts On File, 2002.

"Lute Olson Biography." CoachLuteOlson.com. Retrieved June 10, 2007 (http://www.coachluteolson.com/bio.html).

"The Origin of 'Huskies.'" GoHuskies.com. 2007. Retrieved June 15, 2007 (http://gohuskies.cstv.com/trads/huskies-name.html).

Naismith Memorial Basketball Hall of Fame. "John R. Wooden Enshrined as a Coach in 1973." "Ralph H. Miller Enshrined as Coach in 1988." 2007. Retrieved June 2007 (http://www.hoophall.com/halloffamers/bhof-halloffamers.html).

Schwartz, Larry. "Biography: Kareem Abdul-Jabbar." Retrieved June 12, 2007 (http://www.sportsplacement.com/kareembio.htm).

Shouler, Ken, ed. *Total Basketball: The Ultimate Basketball Encyclopedia*. Wilmington, DE: Sport Media Publishing, 2003.

Sloan, Joanne, and Cheryl Watts. *College Nicknames: And Other Interesting Sports Traditions*. Northport, AL: Vision Press, 1993.

"The Story Behind Bear Down." The University of Arizona. December 4, 2006. Retrieved June 15, 2007 (http://www.arizonaathletics.com/Common/Article.aspx?id=9772).

"UCLA Traditions." UCLA History Project. Retrieved June 15, 2007 (http://www.uclahistoryproject.ucla.edu/Traditions/Home.asp).

USA Basketball. "Jason Kidd." May 23, 2007. "Mike Bibby." February 27, 2004. "#14—Gary Payton." 2001. Retrieved June 2007 (http://www.usabasketball.com/biosmen/bios_listing_men.html).

INDEX

About the Author

Jeremy Harrow has a degree in media and communications. As a former community reporter, Harrow has experience writing about national news from a local perspective. His first college basketball memory was watching his hometown team, St. John's, play in the 1985 Final Four. Harrow lives in New York.

Photo Credits

Cover (top and bottom), pp. 4–5, 9, 20, 25, 30, 31, 35, 37, 39 © Getty Images; pp. 1, 12–13 © www.istockphoto.com/Luis Lotax, p. 3 (left) www.istockphoto.com/Benjamin Goode; pp. 6, 14, 21, 27, 34 © www.istockphoto.com; pp. 8, 11, 17, 23 © AP Photos; p. 15, 22 © Bettmann/Corbis; pp. 19, 28, 33, 38 © Icon Sports Media; p. 24 © Collegiate Images/Getty Images; p. 26 © www.istockphoto.com/Bill Grove.

Designer: Tom Forget
Photo Editor: Marty Levick